OAK TREE ALCHEMY

edited by Brian Clark and Ian Gouge

First published in paperback format by
Coverstory books, 2019

ISBN 978-1-9993027-4-0

www.coverstorybooks.com

Brian Clark

Brian Cuffley

Lydia Ebdon

Ian Gouge

Roger J. Gould

Paul Judge

David McAndrew

Christopher Pearson

Mary Reval

David Smith

Kate Swann

*

Foreword

Oak Tree Alchemy, the title of this poetry collection brought to you by eleven members of The Poetry Society's North Yorkshire group, has a more literal than literary derivation.

The poets meet, read and discuss their work once a month at The Oak Tree Inn, Helperby, a village between Boroughbridge and Easingwold. Their readings and discussions inspire them to write more and better poetry, with all its transformative powers. And they are confident that you will find some gold in the following pages.

The Poetry Society's local groups throughout the UK and elsewhere in Europe are known as Stanzas, and there are almost 100 of them. The North Yorkshire Stanza was formed three years ago and its members range from new writers to published and prize-winning poets. Some members travel up to 50 miles to its meetings, sometimes staying overnight.

A major contribution to the Stanza's popularity must be the luxurious private meeting facility provided by The Oak Tree. The book's title justly reflects this and we are grateful for their continuing support. Nor would we, and hopefully you, be enjoying our first venture into print were it not for the encouragement and skills of my co-editor, Ian Gouge, who first proposed this project and has several poetry books to his own name.

We were saddened to learn of the death of David McAndrew soon after five of his poems had been accepted for this book. It is a fitting tribute to him that we are able to publish these as a lasting memory of his enthusiastic and accomplished contribution to the group.

Brian Clark

The Poetry Society
North Yorkshire Stanza Representative

brianinter@aol.com

Brian Clark

Planting Pigeons

We plant pigeons in holes
each wrapped in soggy newsprint
filled with falsehoods.

Soon they will grow
free to fly
through solitary pines

even though they know
messengers are shot
heroic carriers or not

listening for the drone
of flying pizzas, coke
or maybe bombs.

Some will rub shoulders
with the wisest of the past
sadly turned to stone.

Some will perch
on memorials built to last
like the wars.

Already, the dove-whites
with an olive branch
are in full flight.

Last Seen at Blos Café

Even if it doesn't make a summer
just one would be welcome
but none have come
to wheel and swoop
around the barns and sheds
our red, corrugated hen hut
or ready-made terracotta nests
I put up near some plastic
because young ones slipped off it
the year before last.

I'd taken your return for granted.
Your dipped-wing fly past
every September
in salute to our alliance
as you set out to cross the Sahara
dodge Nigerian nets
skim over jungle
and brush past giraffes in the Veldt
en route from Yorkshire's moors
to Blos Café, Pretoria
where I thought I saw you last Christmas
(well, it's possible).
I miss your line-up:
that unrehearsed dance troupe
wobbling on the wires
preparing for maiden flights.
Your favoured perch, our tv aerial
pointing south, still waits
to receive a missing episode.

Brian Clark

Uncertainties of Norfolk

A borrowed land haunted by water ghosts
who on the tide steal up its mudflat creeks
thwarted by sluice, seawall and ditch
spirits who seem to say here we meet
at this uncertain mix of land and sea
under a sky so big it puts me in my place.
Unsettled waters freed to seek how the land lies
through the sway of reeds, under surveillance
of egret and dragonfly to scratch the silence
of saltmarsh wildness and salt the roots
of aster, sea-lavender and samphire.

    Wade the creek
    note the time
    find the path
    planked over fleet and dyke
    where local kids go
    to mudslide.
    Angle your feet
    tilt the insides up
    don't walk flat
    keep moving
    watch out
    this tide comes in fast.

Followed footprints disappear in the gleam
of a mud-smooth cockle strand and conceal
the only safe way across to Scolt Head Island
and its siren white-sand beaches.

The Pals

Huts full of lads who'd lied about their age
pretending to shave in the stream
learning patriotic songs and the art of war
from those who did not know

laughed with their volunteer pals from Leeds
sighed when they sailed for Suez, not the Western Front
swam in the canal, played football in the sand
then some god of chance shipped them off to France

to be first over the top
in the war to end all wars.
That did not.

The Battle of the Somme
wiped out their battalion
in minutes.
They fell on top of one another,
some left writhing on the wire.

Near their memorial in a dead-end Yorkshire dale
where once a thousand soldier boys
lived off rabbit stew and waited,
lie smithereens of crockery
and an empty beer bottle
outside freshly-dug burrows.

To the sound of gunfire on the moors
an old woman puts a red rose in a vase.
A man in breeches stops his four-by-four
and yanks a dying pheasant from the wire.

Brian Clark

Resurrection

They dug up the dead
and knocked the church down.
We'd sung our last hymn on Sunday
filled to overflowing, in candlelight:
Now the day is over
night is growing nigh
everywhere flattened
and that was the end of West End.
They re-buried the already dead
in a forlorn field of gravestones
high up on Thruscross ridge
to mark a village that died
before its time, sacrificed
to satisfy the cities' thirsts.

But they left the humpback bridge
where we used to watch brown trout
and from the fence that blocked the road
I saw the River Washburn rise
filled to overflowing.

Years later, the reservoir
drained by unforeseen dry seasons
revealed its drowned, knocked-down history.

The bridge rose again
and I crossed it.

Two Cities

I saunter these darkest of streets
past empty temples with glowing intercoms
roam through canyons of night-time aromas
drawn mothlike to lights of welcoming inns
along my dreamline of chance encounters
which ends, as always, in some cul-de-sac
or back at the flat with a stack of coins
to meter the empty night away.

A wail of sirens lures me to docklands
a scent of escape on ships bound for Atlantis.
I sail to an island of thyme-scented crags
where olives twist their roots
in search of water under a distilled sun
on the dried shores of the Mediterranean.

I saunter to the slow, rhythmic rock of cicadas
along an ancient path of golden dust until I pause
at a vanished city's gates and see
revealed by a lizard's dart
the verdigris of ancient coins
worn-away gods to decipher:
my hands in the till of time.

Taking a Walk to Think Things Over

I wandered on the beaten track
while my shadow
long under a sinking sun
strode the riverbank below.
I wondered if it was me down there
waving
or someone else waving back
who could feel the rush of the river
inches away
and as I watched
they waded in and wobbled across
to weeping willows on the other side
then turned and beckoned me to follow.
I chose to stay up on the path
but sensed a shadow somewhere
even when the sun went down
that night of the first frost.

Brian Clark

Brian Cuffley

The Lapwing

Propelled higher and forward by rapid shallow wing-beats
the black and white bird is focused like a springboard diver
whose muscles know the instant to leap
his fluty, warbling chords demanding: look at me
and in a heart-stopping moment

$$f$$
$$a$$
$$l$$
$$l$$
$$s$$

spinning once round
exciting, if not a future mate
the human on the ground;
quick pulse resumed, he climbs again
whirrs over the human, circles and lands
till, with undiminished ardour
he strives again for
spectacular seduction.

Wildness in Small Places

By the centuries-worn trod
where hawthorn shoots and green brambles
reach for the sun's ripening rays
a speckled wood landing in the wild verge
opens her book-page wings
as if for the sun to read.
Amid the aroma of hothouse and grass
a spider twitches, ready for fight or flight
beside a hoard of silk-strung water-pearls
each flaring tungsten-white.

The Nutcracker

How Tchaikovsky entertains
with Arabian, Spanish and Russian cameos
the dance of the reed flutes and waltzing flowers.

How strange the magic that touches the soul –
the pas de deux
the glavnyy muzhchina holding
the prima ballerina high.

More elegant than dancing red-crowned cranes;
their hard work and pain become
whole bodies of grace.

Many dancers smile throughout:
'Smile, it lifts the spirit
if you don't you'll cry.'
Should we watch, when it hurts them so much?
Her entire weight on one point;
heaved so gracefully above his head
blisters, bruises, sprains, back pain;
four days off in forty-seven, income low
unhired by thirty-five – why suffer so?

For their art and audience
and loving dance as life.

As they left in the dark, admiring
ribbons of multi-coloured lights shimmering
on Scarborough's inky waters
did a little Spa Theatre magic go with them?

I only wish I had waved back
when they waved to us
before the curtain fell.

Brian Cuffley

The Spell

Past heather moor
sheep-shorn field and blasted tree
a cart track ruts through old woods
to a sunlit field. A pheasant
herds his hareem there
mindless of the mindful hare.

Then it's into the sun-beaten view –
three long fields encompassed by grand trees –
where sheep, strangely calm
raise their heads with ears at ten to two.

Through a gate to a meadow, golden, wild
ancient woodlands, walls each side
butterflies arise before your tread
to the ripple-swarming beck
then on water, calm and slow
sunlight blooms a veil between
two worlds, above and below.
Light flickers on the bank
earth tang, tree-still
feeling long, long being –
a dragonfly sparrowhawks past.

Lydia Ebdon

Trevor Aqueduct

There was a jumper off the bridge last night
police tape flickered in the breeze
impotent blue lights
pulsed a mute mourning

The sighing policeman
diverted me down
by the old bridge below
prompting dread wonder
of whether I would see him there

Would he lie broken on the rocks
would his last thoughts be
scattered through the shallows or
sprayed and whirling in fragments
making a kaleidoscope of
red and gold and neon green
catching and glinting in a
dance with the evening sunbeams

Festival's wake

The hillsides are desolate with flaccid tents
poles askance as if all were forced to flee.
The breeze takes an occasional tent intact to
float it like a bloated corpse, tumble and stack it
along the fence by the empty recycling bin.

The vastness of the tented landscape diminished us
to a few anonymous ants seeking to salvage from
perhaps a hundred acres of sprawl, trying to follow
the priority the refugee warehouse prescribes:
tents, sleeping bags, mats, saucepans, kettles, wellies,
shoes, clothes, food; but leaving airbeds, duvets, and
almost all the tents that, though to be prioritised,
pitched cheek by jowl, are cumbersome to gather and
sometimes pooed in, and we must leave thousands of
those folding camping chairs that services sell for £5.

I find that bags and clothes left out are often burned
by camp fire embers now dull, eerily sombre as light
fades and last wasps buzz above the background hum.
I feel strangely guilty as I scavenge, try to hit a rhythm
in my microscopic patch, draw each fly sheet back as if
an errant teenager may linger, drag out sleeping bags,
often sodden, they will all be washed, sift through food:
biscuits, bacon, beans, beer cans bulged into fat torpedoes.
Glum, I trundle on and try to sing myself a little song.

Three grim hours and you can barely tell we've been
dropping my last load, I acknowledge another woman's
despair, apologise I can't do more, wash my hands but
disgust sticks. Trekking out, I find the hum's source;

a neat platoon of black-and-yellow bulldozers, hands
disowned on wheels, ravenous gapes tearing, twisting,
snapping, scooping, huge mangled piles of tents and
contents ready to burn or bury. In the scoured wake stand
the Romanians I met coming in, shoulder-to-shoulder now
bin bags in hand, then, on command, they whoop and bend
combing the grass for every last plastic flap or glass shard
plucking out every tent peg till the clearance is done.

Blinds are drawn at the big house
artists just took the stage and played
shops just sell, contractors work to order
parents don't question light loads home.

Young buck

He was prone on the drive
in a bundle of panic, then
seeing us, spasmed to his feet
smacked into the house wall
stilt legs buckled
eyes rolled back and
glazed over, opaque

I grabbed a million years
in your gnarled antler
hugged your ribs and
held you up, your sides heaving
heart pounding with mine

Your eye cleared, I admired
your rich, sleek coat
but your prim muzzle
kept panting foam
Too soon, I loosened you
to heave and crash
brace your head back and
go galloping on your side
completely unstoppable

Next morning
you were still perfect
but light furrows
marked your last run.

Lydia Ebdon

Time

Does time flow
backward on a good day
Stick in eddies under bridges
in moments of horror, or love

Does she gallop fastest
from those who most need her
look back laughing
over her shoulder

Does time ever indulge
any of us
Take pity, to dwell and
rock us in her arms

Or must she end her embrace
callously, tipping us out onto
the slate floor of eternity
before walking away?

My Scribbled Mother

If I drew her
it would be from below
to the angle at which
I remember her

She would be a shaky pencil line
long legs stretched by my perspective
a roughly skirt-shaped outline
and way, way up there
some kind of ball of a head

Hair, she had hair
dark or fair?
I'll go for dark

I will squiggle some on
there, that's it
it must have been like that
roughly on top of her head.

Lydia Ebdon

Raspberries

The trips to the fruit cage were a treat that summer
she'd shuffle over the lawn in flat-footed silence
while I trailed, allowed to hold the bowl.

She plucked the fruits deftly, hands stilled
for a miraculous instant, then back to
trembling as she dropped them in and
mumbled "thank you" through
a dangle of fag ash.

Behind her I would drop my head
to the bowl and drink the scent.
Later the fruits burst sweet
but finished in bristly pips.

Ian Gouge

Passion

where did it go
slipping like rainwater through
cracks   in   the   pavement
a deluge lost
fated to remain nothing   but a memory
a tale to be retold over tea and scones
as if we were just old friends
catching up
not people who were once
        caught out
                by the rain

The Myth of You

look for an inauspicious door
left hand-width ajar
and push
gently
do not knock
gauge with that sixth sense
you never knew you had
the potential of the space
beyond
weigh its dimensions
draft the atmosphere
in charcoal
dark
and finger-smudged
sketch the tension
air-clashed
by the bow-wave of your coming
your intrusion
replaces the unseen
frees the unfelt
an exchange of sorts
while the myth of you
remains outside

Attachment

The house her parents left her was too large,
      the car too old.
To compensate, she filled the house with friends,
      and drove never-ending miles.
To both she gave names,
      'Henry' suiting the car.
Now I wonder if they had been
      her only true friends.

I lived our brief relationship
      as if continually redrafting a poem,
ideals, words and an a blurred self-image
      always between us.
I had wanted the beauty of rhyming couplets
      not seeing she lived her life
as if it were experimental free verse
      strangely staccato;
there was little place for soft edges,
      the ludicrously romantic.

Should it have been a surprise she ended up
      calling Rome her home,
giving parties in a villa's catacombs,
      and living as she always had,
erecting barriers to protect her
      from too much affection?

Gas Street Basin

Forty years   misplaced.
Brushed aside
       like Stuart's glasses branch-snagged
       casually flipped slow-motion
       into canal-dark water at the last-morning tiller
       between here and somewhere else.

Years dissolving   inexplicably
as a gentle wake
       resolves back into nothing but a ripple
       the tried and tested ruse
       of leaving not a trace of our recent passing
       for the silent boats that follow.

In harsh shadows   ghostly
memories dance;
       memories of mooring ropes and narrow bunks
       and pubs now driven from soft focus
       into something they didn't used to be
       trapped in their own navigation.

Barley wine.   Skittles.
Courses charted.
       Uncertain fragments wistfully recalled
       as the unexpected bequest of an unplanned stroll,
       spectres on the Gas Street towpath
       after all these rapidly accelerating years.

Coming Together

Opening the door, she found him
       shrunken, lost, defeated,
and "Poor Mags"
       was the first thing she said.

Then she pulled him in
       as much with her force of will
as the arms that enveloped him,
       that begged him to be still.

Comfort the first thing to offer,
       rousing him, bringing him round,
the rescue of a beached sailor
       whose ship, running aground,

he had abandoned; his life
       left to the fate of the mistress sea,
his body battered, his hopes
       in the wreckage of memory.

Roger J. Gould

Year Music

The east wind sings a sad sicilienne
seeking wires and small spaces
for its soprano song;
laments the loss of a year,
suffering the pangs of birth.
Dawn choruses belong to the hardy
birds prizing the coffined worm.
Traffic beats sharp in the frost
then snow-muted drums on;
distantly dancing, the sword and the morris
presage regeneration.

The school-run galop,
the quick-stepping clinging commuters,
miss the breaking of earth and bud,
the alto notes of nesting hens,
as across the annual seed-bed
all tango to leaf and blossom
in maternal anticipation.

Nestlings copy and fly,
crop heavy fields ripen.
Man waltzes with nature
the tenor ripening in time
to soft sad memories
of slow journeys home.
Summer cools, the eternal choice,
hibernation or migration?

The gentle pavane of Autumn,
lazy as smoke from gathered leaves;
all must be garnered
against bass-deep nights, short days
and midwinter festivals,
their alcoholic sunshine
dispelling the crescendos of the gales
with their carols of celebration.

B-movie Night Flight

Midnight blue window
tiny tethered curtains
frame perfectly permed hair
laced linen daintily dabbing
tears as the engines bellow
and the strings throbbing
fly her away from despair
in her uncreased trousseau.
Over the closing credits
the loving loser blunders
into life's lampposts
as among the edits
the director sunders
all his dreams and ghosts.

The Polar Bear Ring

She brushed the sand from his eyelids
the seaweed from his hair
knew he was not long dead
her eyes skilled in drowned seamen.

Beached too ill to move
by his whaler captain father
she had nursed him the only job
for an half-Inuit pariah.
The next season bringing no whalers
they had married tidying
the settlement's flotsam.

Her ear cold from the draught
through the plank-wall cracks
she had learned
his father's vow
to bring him home
to his wife and children.

Awkwardly he had spoken
of his love of the sea
the whaling his homeland
returning next season
fitted her bone ring
over his finger.

She had waved him away
the polar bear's curse sailing with him
now not on his finger
overwhelmed by the malison of the sea.

Love Song with Locomotives

Even in midsummer it was dark
when they hauled me away from you,
past electricians plotting their downfall,
all the way to Winchester.
They haven't lost their looks,
surgery has kept them young;
our vintage, they look better.
After work, they might escort us
from Waterloo to Wimbledon.
Weary clerks would lift their heads,
smile and point, as they jockeyed with us,
crews firelit, lubricators rocking,
livery glowing green in our carriage lights.
No matter you carried me far away from them,
I loved you all. Their fires will still burn
when, like their smoke, we have gone.

St Cuthbert's Sermon

The brothers who bring me supplies
think I preach, express surprise,
but given time and God's good grace
they'll find this is a blessed place;
that you may be a better flock
than many far beyond this rock.
They understood so little too
but still they said 'amen' like you.
You return on holiday
like family who work away;
my welcome warm as your soft down,
and parishes sharing less, I've known.
When easterlies beat about my cell
I know they batter you as well.
God, whose grace will guide us all,
I pray to let no harm befall
as I commend my ducks to Him
that they may come again to swim
among the rocks where they can fish
for mussels fat, their favoured dish.
When each day we meet, beside the shore,
I ask He bless us, for I am sure
He loves all men, the best and worst,
but at creation, you came first.

Stickmaker

Bob welcomes your hand
age weakens the grip
which skittled out teams
swung the bat
cutting the willow
seeing in hazel
what he coaxed from
young players
now he presses, heats
applies the vice,
tops with ash buffalo ram
polishing embellishing.
On Whernside Rough Tor
Monk's Trod or Caradon
I grip his hand in welcome.

Paul Judge

Belonging

Some twenty years I must have
Cut this same patch of grass
Partially tamed rough pasture
With its lumps and bumps
Never a proper lawn
I must have mown and discarded
Enough grass to raise
A small flock of sheep
If not a cow or two

Edge up close to the hole in the hedge
Often patched, but never mended
Where that dog gets through

Dodge the branches
Carefully up to and round
The few remaining apple trees

There is a contentment to be had
Sitting back to observe
When the job is done
But I sense my real satisfaction
Is in the doing
The physicality
The process

And through the doing
Being part of the place

Waking in the Night

(song lyric)

There's something on your mind
Keeps you waking in the night
Steals the rest out of your sleep-time
From the dark hours through to light
Cruel imaginings, what might-have-beens
The worst that might become
There is no ease from this dilemma
'Til you put down your heavy stone

If you only could decide to take the left or take the right
If you only made the choice, we'd all go forward by your side
Instead of endlessly observing the motion of the tides
Forever circling in the air, never committing to the dive

Fingers clutch at tangled covers
Matted hair, clammy skin
Restless tingling in your veins
Constant pricking doubts within
Caught on the rack of indecision
It's a torment without cease
Resolve shrunk to a whimper
Begging for release

If you only could decide to take the left or take the right
If you only made the choice, we'd all go forward by your side
Instead of endlessly observing the motion of the tides
Forever circling in the air
Circling in the air
Forever circling in the air, never committing to the dive

There's something on your mind
Keeps you waking in the night....

Little Thing

(song lyric)

> Just a little thing
> Just a little thing
> I'd go back and change it if I could
> But the laws of time and space do not allow

If I had looked both ways
If I had chosen different words
Kept my hands deep in my pockets
Thought twice before I cursed

> Maybe that little thing
> Would not have led us to the here and now
> I'd do it different if I could
> But the laws of time and space do not allow

If we could run that scene again
Second take, revised script
With better lighting on the face
Maybe a close-up on the lips
Recast the leading role
Change the location and set
Reshoot the ending of the movie
So there's no cause to regret

> That stupid little thing
> Which led us all to where we are now
> I'd go back and change it in an instant
> But the laws of time and space do not allow

Accepting or declining
A gesture offered or held back
A sentence thought but left unsaid
To do nothing or to act
A single frozen moment
The point where paths divide
All other doors forever closing
Before the ink has dried

And that one little thing
Set the course to our here and now
I'd go back and change it if I could
But the laws of time and space do not allow

Just a little thing
It seemed such a little thing
It was just a little thing
But the aftershocks
are written
large

Distance

How best shall I measure the distance between us
Should I count miles by the hundreds, or flight times in hours
Perhaps think of days, weeks, months, since our last

conversation

Or email, or letter, is it my turn or yours

Could I try to weigh the feelings of longing
The missing of friends, now spread far apart
Or the guilt pangs that come with the realisation
It must be two years since we walked in the hills

Should I count in reverse, as with anticipation
Numbered days become hours 'til my loved one's return
And how to include in this crude calculation
That select band, once few, but ever growing in number
Who live now in our hearts, and in daily recall

Whatever the units, whatever the sum
The true length will never be numbered
There are people who know me, daily acquaintances
Whom in an instant I could reach out and touch
But who are not as close, in the ways that matter
As those good friends, near and far, far and near

David McAndrew

Four Swans

Four swans, their image mirrored on the still
water. Nothing moves. An empty sky
profiles a scatter of trees on a distant hill
and sharpens the far-off bird's intrusive cry.

Clattering, the swans abandon the lake.
They beat their great white wings, and lift themselves
up into lightness, urgent to forsake
the clumsiness of water. This miracle gift

of swift, acquired elegance, leaves them free
to fix direction, test how they might fly;
helps them re-shape their broken geometry
into a fluent line scribed on the sky.

Elegance and force – each has its place
in turning clumsiness to fluency and grace.

Incarnations

The world's a place
for people to make love in
and to die.

And for divinity,
they say,
to try on a mortal face.

And thus, as told in ancient tales,
the urgent need of gods
to put on imperfection.

The deities themselves, it seems,
rage and sigh in vain
for mortal loveliness.

Here we have Danaë
wrapped by the gentle Zeus
in a shower of golden rain.

So Daphne, a water nymph,
escapes divine Apollo's grasp
to be transformed into a laurel tree.

Persephone, daughter of Nature itself,
taken by the King of Hell,
produces spring's beautiful calamity.

They also say
that in the human Christ
the Word was made flesh.

David McAndrew

68

The Alchemy of Grief

Loss is the circumstance in which I lie.
You closed your eyes and turned your head away.
The final choice in which all choices die.

We lay together, watched your life go by.
Living in memories, attempting to delay
that final choice in which all choices die.

You turned away from life. All choices died
in this last choice. There's nothing more to say.
Loss is the circumstance with which I must comply.

Now, without your help, I have to try
to put my hurt on hold, prepare to lay
aside that choice in which all choices die.

Sixty years ago we vowed to try
to live and grow our lives together. Now I pay.
Loss is the circumstance in which I lie.

Now you are gone away I cannot cry.
Grief has expended all I have to say.
Loss is the circumstance in which I lie,
the final choice in which all choices die.

The Rule of Benedict

A modern visitors' centre:
recruitment to the National Trust,
the sale of decorous cards and cashmere scarves,
toilets and restaurants.

With fine views of the abbey,
a discovery trail for children,
picnics on the grass,
the walking of dogs on leads.

Tall, empty arches
admit to pleasing views, with ready access
to this holy place,
once walked by white-cloaked monks.

Within, flagstones and broken walls
clutter the cropped and level lawn.
A paved space, a lapsed altar
and, above, a Green Man.

The age-old Benedictine dispensation
with its formal diagram of prayer
matins, lauds, vespers, compline
today has been displaced.

Now only rooks'
raw, illiterate calls
like black commas
punctuate the yellow sandstone face.

David McAndrew

Fallen stones, like stops and colons,
lie about between the site
and the sandstone face:
a serious archaeology of faith.

Toussaint

to Anne

At Toussaint, mourners
return to La Plancade
from Montauban, from Paris,
everywhere

and gather in the church.
They walk out to the cimetière
carrying chrysanthemums,
yellow and white.

That day, they say,
as flowers flare and flicker
in the cold November light
the talkative dead themselves

walk directly out
through the boundary wall
past the big chestnut trees
and into the shuttered houses.

Yesterday's clogs still echo on the cobbles.
Among rumours of disembodied laughter
a taped accordion tune spins out
its dance in the old, local dialect.

Distant relics of several wars
and broken or unspoken conversations
shape and re-shape what's past
and what's to come.

David McAndrew

And today in this place
the hurt of your death is framed
within fragments like this
of our own and of our neighbours' histories.

Here, where every year
swallows quarrel in the abandoned barn,
I hear lost whispers
of the touch and cry of love.

David McAndrew

Christopher Pearson

Moment of Now

just now

every part of me is intent on demonstrating

my attentiveness to a harrogate buddhist

he is in red and yellow robes having

a soothing tone

i have taken off my shoes

i am sitting my eyes are closed

and i am focusing as suggested

while my thoughts find

monday week

and a necessity now comes into mind

> Captivated in childhood, as i was
> By the stories of Noggin the Nog
> For me an impressionable time
> Back in 1959
> It explained to me, almost everything
> In Episode 1, *The King.*
>
> > *In the lands of the north, where the black rocks*
> > *stand guard against the cold sea, in the dark night that is very*
> > *long, the men of the northlands sit by*
> > *the great log fires and they tell a tale.*

now i notice everyone else

has opened their eyes

and they are talking

about going for lunch

Masking Unusuality

SLOW BEATING WINGS A SEEKING HERON HEADING RIGHT
INTO THE WEST ACROSS RUTLAND OUT TOWARDS ITS
WATER AND THE SUN PINK ACROSS THE TREETOPS THEN
FLICKERING THROUGH HEDGES

THE A1 BEING THE VEIN FLOWING BACK TOWARDS THE
SOUTH AND DRAINING DOWN TO A RUDIMENT OR
DISCOVERY FROM A TIME UNREMEMBERED NOW

A LIKENESS SINCE DEBASED BY TRAVESTY SEEN PERHAPS
BY BETJEMAN YET UNREPORTED IN NOOKS AND CORNERS
OF THE NEW BARBARISM YOU LIVED IN SLOUGH AND
BOUGHT PRIVATE EYE ON SUBSCRIPTION EVEN THEN NEVER
SENDING THE GIFTED CHRISTMAS CARDS BUT SAVOURING
THEIR UNKIND HUMOUR PAMPERING YOUR OWN SMOOTH
WARM FLESH WITH POTIONS AND YOUR IMAGINATION WITH
LONG WHISPERED NIGHTTIME STORIES WHILE OFFERING
YOUR WHOLE SELF TO ANYONE WHO WOULD CARE
ENOUGH TO SHARE A WORTHLESS INTIMACY IN MOMENTS
EVENINGS BENEATH A BERKSHIRE BLUE SKY BOUNDED AT
THE WINDOW OUT ACROSS THE MUDDY FLATS AND
BEYOND THE ELEVATED EXPRESSWAY TO ETON WICK
WHERE YOUR MOTHER STILL LIVES IN THE FAR DISTANCE
BEYOND THE TREES

At the Beginning of an Impossibly Long Day

At the very far edge of this concrete floor
a tired policeman shift-end bleary
       Willkommen in Winterthur
careless clouds cram an unlikely sky
the tree-line silhouetted far behind
and his cooling breakfast waiting
handcuffs to one side

Cold cyclists pass the window one by solitary one

She has chosen
still and elegant
and splashed across her thighs
is everything ever promised
shard sharp now in
another watery dawn beside a lapping lake
like that big wet dog
barking in the grey cemented street

An Evening with Friends

Coming in from the cold
       stepping by the Dansette on its wobbly legs
       playing right there beside that stiff black door
       with the small brass catch loose in its tin lock
the voice saying this now
       in such a small room
       having seven walls of course its window over rooftops
       blow heater and lamp with a silk scarf shade
       a full-length mirror in the alcove
sounding just like Richard Burton speaking out
penetrating smoke as well as lingering dusk
       over here beyond candle light
       a shadow in one of many corners
       the moist proximity
       and a semblance of her perfume as she moves
       closer with intent
his baritone is thinning the music
recounting trivia being his general preference just now
while her fragrance erodes a fragile will.

About Memory

i am
walking down upper edward street
it is about two on a spring afternoon and
> something that i will later describe as a branch
> but which is a twig
> falls from a tree and although it seems to have been
> discarded by a crow
it reminds me
nevertheless
> of this table magician at an otherwise rather formal
> dinner i am attending this autumn
>> who is just now making a wine bottle disappear
>>> through the table
>> and
>> at the same time predicts numbers i will choose on a
>>> die
> which he calls a dice
nevertheless
> the nexus is now a road traffic accident
> happening one evening early in the summer
>> in my home i am recounting a version of it to a visiting
>>> policeman
>> while my then wife gets juice next feeding him
>>> strawberries and cream
>> because it is wimbledon
>> and i am discovering something about
> men with a purpose
> and about women
> too maybe

An Archaeology of Ordinary Things

what we witness here
now
should really be no more
than
an uncovering of much that once
was common knowledge

      questioning rediscovery while admiring its bold
                                  unmasking
      by some sleight of shared awareness in
      what might be
      naturally forgotten
      or simply given up to time

already making a carefully-calibrated measurement
quantifying what
one time
was homely and cherished

where now laser beams straighter than any die
follow lines that once evolved as little more
than the edge that is between two things

      because what has been obscured
      was of course never even hidden
      but it seems however unlikely this may be
      that Earth itself has grown
      and healed around the evidence

Feels Like the First of a Thousand Short Poems: Saturday Evening

walking away from the top lake
heading up towards the obelisk
now stark atop the rise

through the broad evening meadow
predicting a drone of insects in flight
discovering just a whispering breeze

and in the empty blue arching over
expecting swifts swallows and martins

Mary Reval

The Prioress

Snowdrop time again, an early start
of spring. They spread across the grass like shreds
of lace. We planted them here where once our
cemetery was, hoping for eternal life.

My sisters, buried in their shrouds, have long
ago merged into earth. Fast asleep,
they wait for the end of time to come.
For more than five hundred years, I rested

in my stone coffin in their midst until
I was taken away with my tomb
to make room for the sheep and their lambs.
They cemented the casket into the wall

of the priory. Now I have to stand
upright behind my funeral slab.
Sometimes, under a starless sky, I slip
out of my prison, glide over the field

to join all the others in the paddock.
Six of my flock are missing. They were sent
home to their families during King Henry's
dissolution, were interred far away.

The other day, there was an argument
in front of me between the woman who
made a garden next to me and a new
man who wanted to tear down my wall.

This would have made me a homeless
soul, a heap of old bones to be thrown away.
I heard the woman speak to the builders,
'The wall is haunted, because of the grave.

Don't touch.' The builders stepped back. It
gave me a bold idea. I summoned all my
remaining strength and dared to make
an appearance in the man's kitchen at night.

This did the trick. I'm now part of a listed
monument, the Keldholme wall. I still have
to stand in my box, but near my sisters.
Soon there will be new lambs in the paddock.

The Waterloo Tree

It will soon be two hundred years
standing here, your six arms raised to heaven
candelabra shape, in recognition
of that great victory at Waterloo.

With those who put you here long gone,
you keep a watch on our nightly dreams.
In silvery winter light your pale trunk gleams.
A filigree of twigs, black lace upon

a soft grey sky, shows nakedness in grace.
Here birds and memories come to roost
on summer evenings when we used
to sit and listen to the pigeon's bass,

the natter of a jackdaw parliament,
the robin's feisty song and human
sun-drenched voices in oblivion
of what had been Napoleon's last stand.

Shells and Pebbles

Shells and pebbles on a windowsill,
one of them a deep-sea snail,
bleached by sun and wind,
bones on an ancient battlefield

playthings of a long lost child,
tiny shells like fingernails,
the snail still singing of the sea,
all placed there by grieving hands

collector's items of a broken soul.
I take a polished pebble,
let it dance across the water
in the sun; it skips from wave to wave

becomes a leaping fish and sparkles
in the spray and plays, full of joy.
Then again it is a stone
drawn by its weight into the ocean's depth

disappearing like a passing thought
of summers under hazy skies,
sinking to the bottom of my mind
where memories live until they rise again.

Bloodstones

Wild rosehips glowing in the dark
dancing naked through the hedge,
bloodstones round the slender neck
of Jezebel, the queen, defying all

those men, dancing in the rain and
singing tunes full lust. Then, at once
Elijah's horses storm towards heaven
and dogs lap up her blood with greed.

Later in the pub, where men do meet,
there sounds a voice: 'we had no choice –
the bitch deserved it. We don't want
strangers here in our promised land.'

A Hint of Spring

A hint of spring is in the air.
Sunrays stroke my hungry skin.
A gentle wind plays with my hair.
Sparrow voices engulf me with their din.

The river is swollen with molten snow.
Its waters gurgle, rush over the weir.
Puddles still stand on the frozen meadow
where sheep huddle in woollen despair.

Snowdrops and aconites shyly raise
their heads to whisper of frosts to come.
Harbingers of death and paradise
in churchyards; keep them out of your home.

Closing my eyes, I drift away in thought
and lose myself in memories of warmer days
until a chilly gust pierces me, fraught
with sudden fear.
                    But the sheep still graze.

Snow

I walk across the stubble fields in snow.
Its fluff is muffling sounds and turns raw
lines into soft down. Without a flaw,
a gentle fall of flakes has spread a throw

for beasts to leave their tracks: a crow
writes runes, a robin spidery script. I saw
the indentations from a big dog's paw.
Fox left a bright red puddle in the snow.

The field in fog, a room in muted glow,
blurred are the shapes of trees and fence,
lying under bridal veils until the cotton wall

of mist is pierced by sunlight's arrow.
The hillside gleams in icy incandescence,
zillions of crystals send a blinding signal:
             NOEL

David Smith

On Seeing a Collapsed Drystone Wall

Squashed rusk crumbs from podgy
High-chair fingers deliberately
Dribbling.

Frustrated tears leeching from
A childhood spilt jigsaw just
Before the howl and
Explosion of your teenage room.

Its belts, shirts and skirts
Cascading from stepping stone wardrobe drawers
Mingling with the scree of underwear, compact discs
Experimental lipsticks.

A rubble of bottles and half-finished essays
Spilling across your student's throbbing floor
Closed curtains hide you
After he said he was leaving.

Cameraria Ohridella

Is a leaf mining moth that can't fly
So has hitched lifts on lorries and cars
All the way from Macedonia, finally finding
My boyhood chestnut tree.

It stands in Joe Wilson's former farmyard
Where he kept a cow, a sow and a few hens
Opposite the bulge in the church wall.

After Sunday school we hid amongst leaves bigger
Than our heads, and dropped conkers on choir girls.

Today is the first of August, autumn has come early.
Her once magnificent spars, stark as the Somme
Are bare, black against blue.

A retired executive is sweeping
Shrivelled brown-edged fingers
Into his bright red wheelbarrow and
Trundling my childhood away.

David Smith

Sunday Morning Market in Estepona

A double-bent old man
weaves apologetically through
the cross-currents of tourists,
who clutch their wallets
who look away, at their feet.

He hops on his good leg,
his other withered, flops, footless.

Sweeping his crutch
in an arc learnt from childhood
he holds a plastic cup from Starbucks.

Quiet as light, the Somali boy slips
from behind his furtive pile of leather bags,
belts, an eddy of watches, his knuckle of
fake Ray-Bans.

Coins clatter on plastic.

The Biro From "The Nymphe Brasserie"

A freebie memento of the night spent
in that lanky Dutch hotel.

Clinging to rope banisters
we giggled up vertical stairs
to our attic room,
bar-buzz seeped
through the planked floor.

You were marooned in the enormous hip bath.

The stern iron bedstead was softened
by Mexican throws.

We were making notes on MacNeice's poem 'Meeting Point'

-   Time was away and somewhere else,
-   There were two glasses and two chairs
-   and two people with one pulse

When you ran out.

I kept hoping, trying
until someone whispered
"This one isn't working".

Prognosis

Can I kiss it better, like a scraped knee
a nettled leg,
it is all I can think of
it has always worked before.

I don't want to think about your storm coming
into our secret field of flowers
your words tumbling out of their barracks
in strange uniforms, their boots trampling
the corners of our blanket
spilling, staining and spreading.

I look down our favourite lane
the one you said the trees hold hands
and see the fact barricades
already manned.

The first waves of inevitability
are advancing, as gently as you can
you say
"We have to leave now"

For a clinical assessment
of our lives.

Namib Desert

They said it was beautiful
The desert an ocean of silence, surely
this is eternity, a solemn oath to the sunrise
carving its scriptures on the ancient dunes.

How simple termites led man
to scrabble to find diamonds in this vastness
how a bushman's woman must leave
one of her twins behind.

The curved horizons, omniscient moons
demanding full confession to something beyond.

So it was no surprise that you had left the long table
growing with noise and swaying steins.

I followed your trail of discarded chattels
to the silence of your acacia.
After a long time
you spoke:
"I now feel beautifully irrelevant,
as if I am stripped, pared like the skeleton
of that gemsbok on the fence-line.
If I have been on this Earth before
it was here, If I come back
meet me".

The Reading

After they had heard my poems
they said nothing.

Held me in a suspension
of silence so severe it sucked
the air from the room.

Perhaps embarrassed by
my lack of talent they looked away
could only mouth in whispers.

Or did I cause a squirm, transmit
a fever leaving shivers
in intimate places.

Maybe a word skewered the truth
picked locks to compartments, a
phrase breached their facade, invaded dreams
releasing raw echoes of lost voices
exposed joyous tangled bodies
the blushing fragments of mistakes
we all possess.

No matter for the b..........
they said nothing.

Kate Swann

Lost Settlement at Kitridding

Deep down under my feet
the bones of the village lie quietly
sunk into the rich loam of the hillside
long forgotten names unbidden
by those who pass in a hurry.

West wind carries the song you sang
to your children cradled in sheepskin
sheltered from the ice sharp blast
long before wood was fashioned
nailed and painted for cots.

As winter sun breaches slate clouds
I think I glimpse your shadow foraging
for berries in the shrubs and bushes
filling skins with pure spring water
in ways you learned from your mother.

Needles on the trees rattle as if
disturbed by ghosts of hunters
running through the wolven forest
lit by a lazy fading moon
in pursuit of fleeing prey.

You are not meant to be seen
but remain hidden   potent
a link between history and present
revealing just a skeleton of stones
ritual patterns in hollows of earth.

Kate Swann

In The Ring

It's a mental game as you raise your glove
there's no room for fear, feel the strength
of the smell of rust in another man's blood

No limits, no stopping, is it like love
as you feel his force when your bodies clinch
in a mental game as you raise your glove

The cut on his eye oozing a warm flood
makes cold sweat on your brow, you inhale breath
with an odour of rust from this man's blood

Fist in, jabbing thrust, shoulders meet and shove
feet dance to and fro, a quick-fire agile path
in a mental game as you raise your glove

Bell rings, a moments rest, water tastes good
to a poser drowning the acid in his mouth
from a stench of rust in another man's blood

You just have to stay and take the beating
no half measures, gladiators meeting
in a mental game as you raise your glove
to the smell of rust, it's another man's blood

Prompted by Chris Eubank's comment "You just have to stay and take the beating".

Charades

We were never still   never quiet
conversations started by one
finished by the other
interrupted
never quite completed
but always laughing
through the school run
shopping   cricket teas
even when you moved away

Now the distance is a chasm
suspended in silence
eyes filled with fear
a word jumbles
earnestly from your lips
with no form
frustration in your stricken body
desperately fighting
to move words from your head
to your mouth   to me

How can I translate
the monotone sound
filled with desperation
will the long game we play
bring understanding
across this void
wider than I can measure
though I can see your face
hold your hand   bring you tea

Kate Swann

Layers

It was a Sunday   which meant
nothing when the day was sweet
and the hedge needed laying
he held no truck with tractors
tearing tender spears raw   dripping sap
through spikes of twigs frayed like torn cloth.

He says the skill is in the eye
not in the strength of an arm
a cut in the right place laid to the sun
gives the pleacher new life to be
tomorrow's stem for flower and fruit
let wildlife pass through the smeuse.

The tools had been his fathers
each one hanging   oiled and sharp
on carefully aligned hooks in the shed
battle ready   glinting in the light
waiting for the heavy dew to lift
with the skylarks in early warmth.

He lays his hands gently along
the hawthorn trunk measuring
the right height to place the cut
the shape of his father's fingers
dented in the handle   the billhook
falls through the air   startling sparrows.

Samba Café, Lisbon

How easily the women slip
into the men's arms
stranger or lover locked
from rib-cage to thigh   swaying
to the beat of the boom-box samba
on the floor of the street café

How easily the young men
slide on and off the dance floor
changing partners with a smile
learn a step   show a move
bewitch the audience   then
drift away into the lazy heat

How easily the old man
sheds the mantle of infirmity
clasps his partner's hands and
with hypnotic lightness
rocks his shoulders   rolls his hips
claims the space for his sorcery

We sit and drink coffee in
white cups and saucers
tap our feet nonchalantly
to the rhythm   moving our bodies
preparing to join the dance
but choosing not to   just yet

Packing Up

after Niall Campbell

Yes that is my suitcase by the door
destination written loudly on the label
sadness
                          shaken out then neatly folded
slipped tightly in-between my cotton shirts
feelings pressed
                          flattened and zipped
into my wash bag with soothing creams
a growing sense of loss
                          twisted in pink tissue
tucked into my shoes with woolly socks
a winter coat
                          I'll wear my mac
with hankie in the pocket
memories begin to disintegrate
like the tickets
                          curled within my sweaty hands
the straps hold down a rising breath of anger
as defiance presses up against the lid
suitcase firmly locked
                          the travelling begins

The Shift of Time

We sidle down the main street
strut mascara and mini skirts
too old for the playground
too young for the pub

impatience thrums through our bodies
as the clock in the tower ticks
away the minutes too slowly
in our need to be grown up

we make do with a game of table tennis
rivalry runs through every move
as we tack to and fro either side of the table
one eye on the ball   the other on the boys

we drift back along the lane
stop to watch a game of bowls
laugh in the certainty that we
will never be so slow   so bent   so old

as if to prove this we run
to sit on the fish shop wall
share a portion of chips and watch
ghosts emerge from the works van

diatomite dust on each tired face
white dynamite in weary lungs
widows in waiting make cups of tea
for men already in decline

Acknowledgements

- **Last Seen at Blos Café** by Brian Clark, previously published in *Poet of the Year 2016*, Canterbury Festival.
- **Resurrection** by Brian Clark, was published in *Poetry News*.
- **Two Cities** by Brian Clark, appeared in *Deus Loci*, journal of The International Lawrence Durrell Society.
- **Passion, The Myth of You, Attachment,** and **Gas Street Basin** by Ian Gouge were previously published in *First-time Visions of Earth from Space* (Coverstory books, 2019).
- **Coming Together** by Ian Gouge was previously published in *After the Rehearsals* (Coverstory books, 2018).
- **The Prioress** by Mary Reval appeared in *Writing 13*, Sheffield Hallam University.
- **Cameraria Ohridella** by David Smith was first published in *The Stencil Room* (Sixth Element Publishing).
- **Prognosis** by David Smith was in *Unnatural Workings* (Quoin Publishing Ltd.).
- **Layers** by Kate Swann was published in *This Place I Know: a Cumbrian Anthology* (Hatstand Press).
- **A Shift in Time** by Kate Swann appeared in Speakeasy magazine.

Lightning Source UK Ltd.
Milton Keynes UK
UKHW012326080319
338799UK00005B/40/P